Chicago
SKY

by Charlie Beattie

Copyright © 2026 by Press Room Editions. All rights reserved. No part of this book may be used or reproduced in any manner whatsoever, including internet usage, without written permission from the copyright owner, except in the case of brief quotations embodied in critical articles and reviews.

Book design by Kate Liestman
Cover design by Kate Liestman

Photographs ©: Shaina Benhiyoun/Sports Press Photo/Sipa USA/AP Images, cover, 25; Melissa Tamez/Icon Sportswire/AP Images, 4, 7, 27; Geoff Stellfox/Getty Images Sport/Getty Images, 8; Thearon Henderson/AP Images, 10; Michael Conroy/AP Images, 13; Leon Bennett/Getty Images Sport/Getty Images, 15; John Bazemore/AP Images, 16; Christian Petersen/Getty Images Sport/Getty Images, 19; Meg Oliphant/Getty Images Sport/Getty Images, 20; Michael Reaves/Getty Images Sport/Getty Images, 22, 29

Press Box Books, an imprint of Press Room Editions.

ISBN
979-8-89469-010-0 (library bound)
979-8-89469-023-0 (paperback)
979-8-89469-048-3 (epub)
979-8-89469-036-0 (hosted ebook)

Library of Congress Control Number: 2025930843

Distributed by North Star Editions, Inc.
2297 Waters Drive
Mendota Heights, MN 55120
www.northstareditions.com

Printed in the United States of America
082025

ABOUT THE AUTHOR

Charlie Beattie is a writer, editor, and former sportscaster. Originally from Saint Paul, Minnesota, he now lives in Charleston, South Carolina, with his wife and son.

TABLE OF CONTENTS

CHAPTER 1
DOUBLE-DOUBLE MACHINE   **5**

CHAPTER 2
A SLOW START   **11**

CHAPTER 3
A BIG DEAL   **17**

CHAPTER 4
SKY'S THE LIMIT   **23**

SUPERSTAR PROFILE
COURTNEY VANDERSLOOT   **28**

QUICK STATS   30
GLOSSARY   31
TO LEARN MORE   32
INDEX   32

CHAPTER 1

DOUBLE-DOUBLE MACHINE

Chicago Sky guard Lindsay Allen had the ball beyond the three-point line. Allen dribbled around a screen set by center Kamilla Cardoso. Then Cardoso rolled to the basket.

The Sky were facing the Seattle Storm in the 2024 Women's National Basketball Association (WNBA)

Lindsay Allen averaged 3.9 assists per game in 2024.

regular season. Midway through the third quarter, the Sky trailed the Storm 47–42. Allen fired a pass to Cardoso. The rookie attempted an open layup. But her shot bounced off the rim. Angel Reese prepared for the rebound. The rookie forward grabbed the ball and banked it in.

Reese didn't make a fancy play. But the bucket made WNBA history. The shot gave Reese 11 points, which secured a double-double. Reese had posted at least 10 points and 10 rebounds for the 13th straight game. No WNBA player had ever done that before.

Legendary forward Candace Parker had set the old record in 2010. Reese's

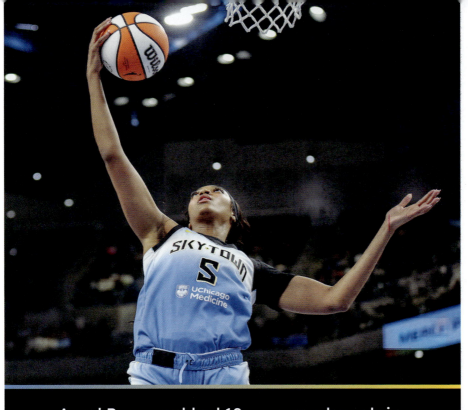

Angel Reese grabbed 10 or more rebounds in 29 of 34 games in 2024.

WNBA career was just getting started. But she was already one of the league's most exciting players.

The Sky ended up losing to Seattle 84–71. But Reese finished the game with 17 points and 14 rebounds. Three nights later, she posted another double-double.

Reese averaged 13.6 points per game in 2024.

The Sky beat the Atlanta Dream 78–69. Reese then recorded 10 points and 10 rebounds in Chicago's next game. Reese's streak had reached 15 games.

Other players admired Reese's toughness and consistency. WNBA legend

Teresa Weatherspoon coached the Sky in 2024. She said Reese was amazing.

Reese's streak ended on July 13. But she continued to impress for the rest of the season. She finished the year with an average of 13.1 rebounds per game. The next closest player averaged 11.9. Few rookies had adjusted to the league quicker than Reese. Sky fans couldn't wait to see what their young star would do next.

SHORT-LIVED RECORD

Reese finished her rookie season with 446 total rebounds. That broke the old record of 404. She didn't keep the record for long, though. An injury forced Reese to miss the last six games of the year. Las Vegas Aces center A'ja Wilson passed Reese late in the season. Wilson finished with 451 rebounds.

CHAPTER 2

A SLOW START

The Chicago Sky took the court for the first time on May 20, 2006. The Sky were on the road facing the Charlotte Sting. With one second to play, Chicago trailed 82–80. Guard Jia Perkins drew a foul while shooting a three-pointer. Perkins stepped up to the line and sank all three free throws. Chicago earned a thrilling 83–82 win.

Jia Perkins averaged 12.5 points per game during her five seasons with the Sky.

Three days later, the Sky held their home opener. More than 5,100 fans cheered them on. The Sacramento Monarchs stole the spotlight, though. They beat Chicago 76–63. Losses piled up during the Sky's first season. The team finished 5–29.

It took several years for Chicago to put a winning team on the court. The Sky suffered losing records in each of their first seven seasons. Those tough

AN INDEPENDENT TEAM

Until 2002, each WNBA team was tied to the National Basketball Association (NBA) team in its city. Chicago's NBA team is the Bulls. However, the Sky had nothing to do with the Bulls. The Chicago Sky were the first WNBA team formed without any help from the NBA.

Sylvia Fowles averaged 9.8 rebounds per game while she played with Chicago.

years resulted in high draft picks. Slowly, the Sky added talent. In 2008, the team drafted Sylvia Fowles. The center became one of the league's best rebounders. The Sky added high-scoring guard Epiphanny Prince in 2010. One year later, Chicago drafted Courtney Vandersloot. The point guard showcased incredible vision.

In 2013, the Sky drafted star forward Elena Delle Donne. They finally had all the pieces of a winning team. Delle Donne averaged 18.1 points per game. She won the league's Rookie of the Year Award. That same season, the WNBA named Fowles the Defensive Player of the Year. Chicago finished 24–10. No team in the Eastern Conference had a better record.

In the first round of the playoffs, Chicago faced the Indiana Fever. The Fever had much more experience. They also played physical basketball. Chicago struggled to keep up. Indiana swept the series. Just like that, the Sky's magical season came to an end. But better days were ahead.

Elena Delle Donne played in the All-Star Game in her first three seasons with the Sky.

CHAPTER 3

A BIG DEAL

The Sky made it back to the playoffs in the 2014 season. Their first-round series went to a deciding Game 3. Chicago trailed Atlanta by 17 points in the fourth quarter. Then Elena Delle Donne took over. She scored 34 points in the game. Her last basket came with only 8.2 seconds

Delle Donne celebrates hitting a late shot in a 2014 playoff game against the Atlanta Dream.

left. The superstar's jump shot lifted the Sky to an 81–80 win.

In the semifinals, Chicago lost Game 1 to the Fever. In Game 2, the Sky trailed by 14. This time, Sylvia Fowles led the comeback. She scored 27 points. The Sky won 86–84 in double overtime. Chicago then won Game 3 to reach the WNBA Finals. There, they ran out of rallies. The Phoenix Mercury swept the Sky to win the championship.

In 2015, Delle Donne earned the WNBA Most Valuable Player (MVP) Award. She led the team to a 21–13 record that year. But the Sky's season ended quickly. In the first round of the playoffs, they lost to Indiana in three games.

Fowles averaged 16.2 points per game during the 2014 playoffs.

Delle Donne had another strong year in 2016. However, she asked for a trade after the season. The superstar needed to move closer to her hometown in Delaware. Her sister, Lizzie, lived there. The pair had a close relationship. Lizzie

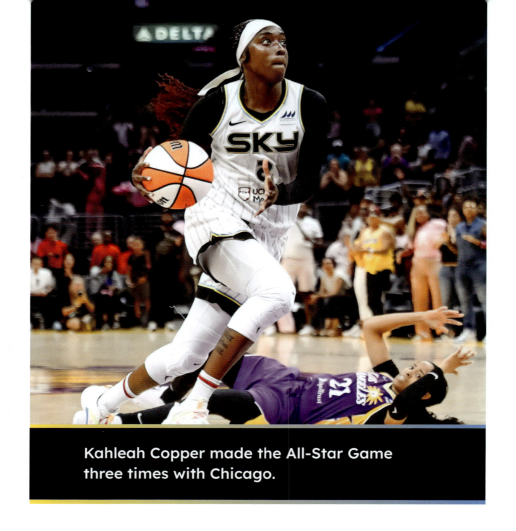

Kahleah Copper made the All-Star Game three times with Chicago.

was blind and had cerebral palsy. She couldn't travel to Chicago for games.

The Sky understood. They traded Delle Donne before the 2017 season. In return, Chicago received two strong players from the Washington Mystics. Forward Kahleah

Copper had great scoring potential. And center Stefanie Dolson played strong defense.

The pair teamed up with an All-Star backcourt. Courtney Vandersloot racked up assists. And Allie Quigley knocked down three-pointers. New coach James Wade led the Sky to the playoffs in 2019 and 2020. Both years, the team came up short. The Sky needed one more star to put them over the top.

SKY GUY

The Sky's original mascot was named Sky Guy. The team described him as the biggest fan of women's basketball in the city. The fictional mascot's story also mentioned he had five older sisters who all played basketball. The team retired Sky Guy in 2024. That year, Chicago replaced him with Skye the Lioness.

CHAPTER 4

SKY'S THE LIMIT

Los Angeles Sparks superstar Candace Parker grew up just outside of Chicago. Before the 2021 season, she signed with her hometown team as a free agent. The Sky saw Parker as the missing piece of the team's puzzle.

Parker led the Sky in rebounding in 2021. Only Kahleah Copper averaged

Candace Parker averaged 13.3 points and 8.4 rebounds per game in 2021.

more points for the team. With talented scorers around her, Courtney Vandersloot led the WNBA in assists.

Chicago struggled in the regular season. Multiple players missed games with injuries. But the Sky were healthy in the playoffs. They won two single-elimination games easily. Then they beat the Connecticut Sun in the semifinals. Chicago returned to the Finals to face the Mercury.

The teams split the first two games. Copper then lit up Game 3 with 22 points. Chicago won 86–50. They needed one more win to secure the title.

With 41 seconds left in Game 4, the Sky led 76–74. After dribbling around a

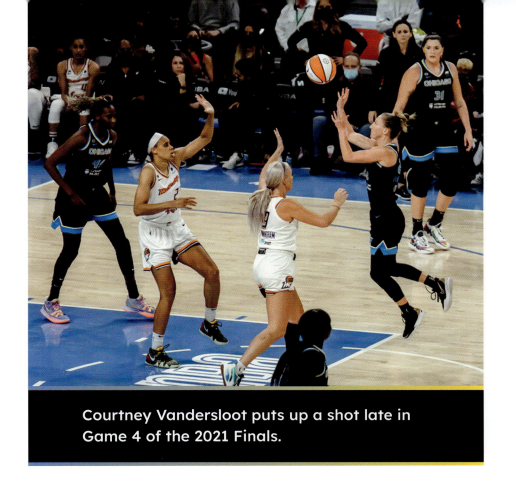

Courtney Vandersloot puts up a shot late in Game 4 of the 2021 Finals.

screen, Vandersloot stopped in the middle of the paint. The point guard had already racked up 15 assists. Instead of passing, Vandersloot looked to shoot. She faked a shot and fooled two defenders. Then she dropped in a fadeaway jumper with 23 seconds to go.

DISHING IT OUT

Courtney Vandersloot took her passing skills to the next level in the 2021 playoffs. In 10 postseason contests, she averaged 10.2 assists per game. In a win against the Sun in the semifinals, Vandersloot dished out 18 assists. That set a WNBA record for most assists in a playoff game.

Vandersloot later sank two free throws to ice the game. Parker fought back tears as Vandersloot stood at the foul line. The Sky had finally won the WNBA title!

In 2022, the team didn't slow down. The Sky set a team record with 26 wins. However, Chicago fell early in the playoffs. Both Parker and Vandersloot left the team after the season ended. Chicago needed to rebuild.

The Sky had two picks in the first round of the 2024 draft. They used

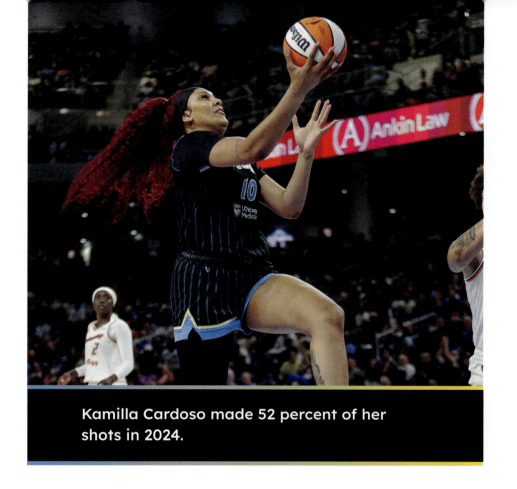

Kamilla Cardoso made 52 percent of her shots in 2024.

their first pick on Kamilla Cardoso. She had just won a championship with the University of South Carolina. Chicago then picked Angel Reese. In 2023, she had led Louisiana State University to a title. Sky fans hoped this duo could someday deliver another championship to Chicago.

SUPERSTAR PROFILE

COURTNEY VANDERSLOOT

No one has played in more games for the Sky than Courtney Vandersloot. The team drafted her with the third pick in 2011. The guard played with Chicago for more than a decade.

Vandersloot had a reliable jump shot. But her passing ability was what stood out most. Vandersloot constantly set up her teammates to score. In 2017, she averaged 8.1 assists per game. No WNBA player had done that before. Vandersloot increased that average each of the next three seasons. In 2020, she became the first WNBA player to average 10 assists per game.

Vandersloot always looked for open teammates. She passed best when the stakes were highest. During the 2021 Finals, she recorded at least 10 assists in all four games. Her vision helped the Sky win their first title.

Vandersloot averaged 6.6 assists per game over her 12 seasons with the Sky.

QUICK STATS

CHICAGO SKY

Founded: 2006

Championships: 1 (2021)

Key coaches:
- Steven Key (2008-10): 42-60
- Pokey Chatman (2011-16): 106-98, 7-12 playoffs
- James Wade (2019-23): 81-59, 13-8 playoffs, 1 WNBA title

Most career points: Allie Quigley (3,723)

Most career assists: Courtney Vandersloot (2,386)

Most career rebounds: Sylvia Fowles (1,832)

Most career steals: Courtney Vandersloot (457)

Most career blocks: Sylvia Fowles (376)

Stats are accurate through the 2024 season.

GLOSSARY

cerebral palsy
A group of disorders that affect a person's balance and ability to move.

double-double
When a player reaches 10 or more of two different statistics in one game.

draft
An event that allows teams to choose new players coming into the league.

fadeaway
A shot taken while moving away from the basket.

free agent
A player who can sign with any team.

paint
The area between the basket and the free-throw line.

rookie
A first-year player.

screen
When an offensive player blocks a defender to create space for a teammate.

TO LEARN MORE

Hanlon, Luke. *Everything Basketball*. Abdo Publishing, 2024.
O'Neal, Ciara. *The WNBA Finals*. Apex Editions, 2023.
Whiting, Jim. *The Story of the Chicago Sky*. Creative Education, 2024.

MORE INFORMATION

To learn more about the Chicago Sky, go to **pressboxbooks.com/AllAccess**. These links are routinely monitored and updated to provide the most current information available.

INDEX

Allen, Lindsay, 5–6
Atlanta Dream, 8, 17

Cardoso, Kamilla, 5–6, 27
Charlotte Sting, 11
Connecticut Sun, 24, 26
Copper, Kahleah, 20–21, 23–24

Delle Donne, Elena, 14, 17–20
Dolson, Stefanie, 21

Fowles, Sylvia, 13–14, 18

Indiana Fever, 14, 18

Las Vegas Aces, 9
Los Angeles Sparks, 23

Parker, Candace, 6, 23, 26
Perkins, Jia, 11
Phoenix Mercury, 18, 24
Prince, Epiphanny, 13

Quigley, Allie, 21

Reese, Angel, 6–9, 27

Sacramento Monarchs, 12
Seattle Storm, 5–7

Vandersloot, Courtney, 13, 21, 24–26, 28

Wade, James, 21
Washington Mystics, 20
Weatherspoon, Teresa, 9
Wilson, A'ja, 9